To mum,

Tha[nk]
the[...]
for
wha[...]
Thank [...] for
always being
there for me and
always making
sure I know you
Love me. You
are very special
and I couldn't
wish for a better
mum + friend.

Love you to
forever
+ Beck
x x x

With special thanks
To Martin Kerr and Amy Schneider for beautiful book design.
To Helen Exley for believing in my work and your constant wise
counsel throughout this project.
To my husband Jim, for everything.
Dedication: To my dear Mother

Published in 2002 by Exley Publications Ltd in Great Britain.
16 Chalk Hill, Watford, Herts WD19 4BG, UK

Published in 2003 by Exley Publications LLC in the USA.
185 Main Street, Spencer, MA 01562, USA

www.helenexleygiftbooks.com

12 11 10 9 8 7 6 5 4 3 2 1

Copyright © Susan Squellati Florence 2002.

The moral right of the author has been asserted.

ISBN 1-86187-418-9

Edited by Helen Exley. Printed in China.

Written and illustrated by Susan Squellati Florence

Helen Exley Giftbooks cover the most powerful of all human
relationships: love between couples, the bonds within families and
between friends. No expense is spared in making sure that each book
is as thoughtful and meaningful a gift as it is possible to create: good
to give, good to receive. You have the result in your hands. If you
have loved it — tell others! We'd rather put the money into more good
books than spend it on advertising. There is no power on earth like
the word-of-mouth recommendation of friends.

ON THE GIFT OF A MOTHER'S LOVE

For my mother from your daughter
a mother too

WRITTEN & ILLUSTRATED BY

Susan Squellati Florence

A HELEN EXLEY GIFTBOOK

*T*his book is a meditation on the extraordinary gifts that a mother's love brings to our lives. It is a way of thanking our own mother for her love. It is also a reflection upon the treasure of love that we, as mothers, have been entrusted with to give our children.

My own mother was twelve years old when her mother died, leaving a husband, eleven children and the struggles of being poor. Mom cannot remember being held, or hugged, or loved by her mother. This has been a source of sadness for her. But she has always given her three children what she never had... the unconditional, ever-present source of nurturing that a mother's love brings.

This deep and strong, constant source of love that a mother brings her child lasts a lifetime.

Pablo Casals, the world reknowned musician, talked about his mother in his book, **Joys and Sorrows** that he wrote at the age of ninety-three. "I have never known anyone like my mother. Her presence has remained with me throughout the years. It is forty years since my mother died, but she has continued to be my guide. Even now she is with me."

I wrote this book for my mother, Ramona Squellati, on her eightieth birthday. It helped me realize the deep value of both the love I have been given and the love I give my children.

A mother's love is the most precious treasure a child can receive. It is a gift that lasts forever.

I never knew
how much you love me,
until I became a mother.

I never understood
how much a part of your life I am,
until I became
a mother.

I never thought about
how much
you have always done
and always do for me
until I became a mother.

Because I am a mother

I know how deep

and strong,

how special

and sublime

this connection

of love is...

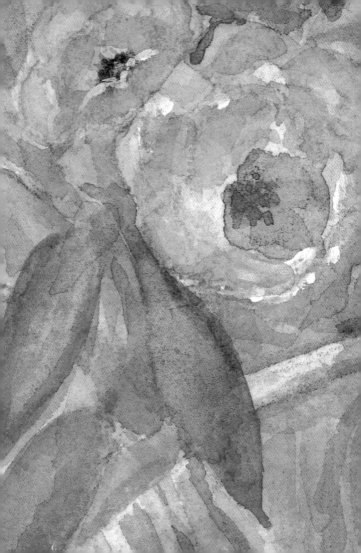

between a mother
and her child.

It is hard to describe
this love you give me.

It is deep

and cannot be measured.

It is never ending,
like the ocean
that goes beyond
the horizon line.

It is evergiving

and replenishing

like the constant flow of water,

from a fountain.

*It is powerful
like electricity
and can light up
one's whole life.*

It is strong enough
to hold on...
and gentle enough
to let go.

Because I am so loved

I am set free

to love others.

Because I am so loved
I am able
to love myself.

Because you believe in me
I can believe
in myself.

Because you listen to me
you let me be me.

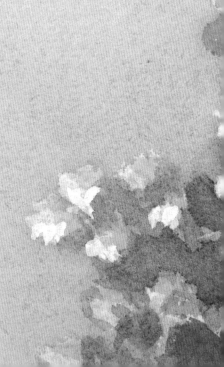

With this love
you have shown me
the grace it takes
to let go of your children,
as they become themselves
and as their lives become
separate from yours.

With this love
you have shown me
the courage it takes
to accept the changes
the years bring...
and the value
of recounting the blessings
these years have brought.

Your love has become within me

a source of strength,

and comfort.

Your love,
like a bouquet of flowers
on the table of my life,

adds joy and beauty

to my everyday.

I am so grateful

to have the gift

of your love,

the gift

...a gift not told in words
but revealed with quiet passion
and constancy
through the days
and the years.

This mothers' love you give me
is the most precious heirloom
I have to give my children.

To be able to give
this gift of love
is an honour I have been
entrusted with.

From hand to hand
and heart to heart...

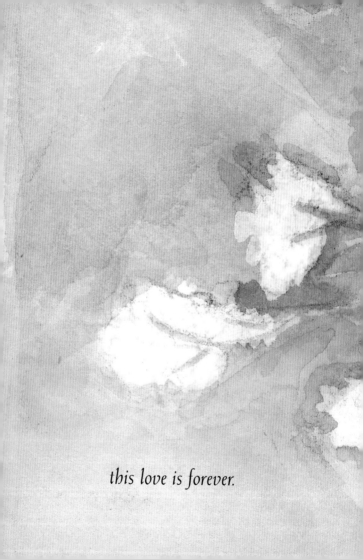

this love is forever.

Thank you for your gift of love.

ABOUT THE AUTHOR

Susan Squellati Florence

The well loved and collected greeting cards of Susan Florence
have sold hundreds of millions of copies in the last
three decades. Her giftbooks have sold over one and a half
million copies.

  With words of gentle wisdom and original paintings, Susan
Florence brings her unique style to all her gift products and
her readers have written time and again to thank her and tell
her how the books were a profound help to them. People have
told Susan that her words speak to them of what they cannot
say... but what they feel.

  Susan Florence's completely new collection of giftbooks in
The Journeys Series invites the readers to pause and look
deeply into their lives. "We all need more time to rediscover
and reflect on what is meaningful and important in our own

lives... and what brings us joy and beauty. Writing these books in The Journeys Series *has helped me understand more fully the value of love and acceptance in helping us through the difficult times as we journey through life."*

Susan lives with her husband, Jim, in Ojai, California. They have two grown children, Brent and Emily.

THE JOURNEYS SERIES

1-86187-420-0
Change... *is a place where new journeys begin*

1-86187-422-7
How wonderful it is... **Having Friends in Our Lives**

1-86187-418-9
On the Gift of A Mother's Love
For my mother from your daughter a mother too

1-86187-419-7
Time Alone *The gift of being with yourself*

1-86187-421-9
When You Lose Someone You Love
...a journey through the heart of grief

1-86187-417-0
Your Journey
...a passage through a difficult time